CONVERSATIONS
From a
QUEST ᶠᴼᴿ DIVINE

My Passion, My Growth, My Transformation

Volume One

Jamaine Wilkins

Order this book online at www.trafford.com
or email orders@trafford.com

Most Trafford titles are also available at major online book retailers.

Printed in the United States of America.

ISBN: 978-1-4669-4174-8 (sc)
ISBN: 978-1-4669-4173-1 (e)

Trafford rev. 08/16/2012

 www.trafford.com

North America & international
toll-free: 1 888 232 4444 (USA & Canada)
phone: 250 383 6864 ♦ fax: 812 355 4082

Contents

DEDICATION

In Loving Memory Of My Mother & Father

Maxine & Charles Wilkins

Peaceful Journey

My grandmother: Emma Ring Davis

My mother: Maxine Wilkins

My father: Charles Earl Wilkins

My cousin: Shelton Porter

My aunt: Mary Alice Porter

My cousin: Leonard Winston

My aunt: Annie May Wright

My great aunt: Helena Armstrong

My great aunt: Eulalee Foster

My uncle: Willie Dan Davis

My great uncle: Wadell Mitchner

My great uncle: Frank Mitchner

My great uncle: Walter Junior Mitchner

My friend: Timothy Farrar

My sister in law: Angie Martinez

My Friend and co worker: Marcellus Farmer

My Friend: Tender (Slingshot) Atturbury

My dog: Binkey

ACKNOWLEDGEMENTS

There are so many people that have aided me on my journey through life to where I am at today. Some have impacted me in ways that they will never know. From family to friends to coworkers, to love ones, to business associates, to mentors, to clients, and to everyone I have encountered on my steps to elevation. I would like to take this time out to say thank you for your push and support. I must always and forever thank God almighty for allowing Jesus Christ to pay the price of sin for me and adopt me as a child of God with access to the inheritance through his will, grace, and mercy. I would like to thank my precious grandmother, Emma Davis, God rest her soul and thank you for starting this wonderful and loving family. Thanks to both my parents, Maxine and Charles, who are on their divine journey. Thanks to my living dad who raised me and was my hero, and mentor, Theodore Pittman. Thanks to my siblings that are all grown up now. My big sister, Beatrice Harrison, my little sisters, Quanisha Rodgers, Charlene Richardson, Nissa Richardson, and my little brother, Charleston Rodgers. To my adorable sons, Dominique Jarrod Wilkins and Dwayne Dominique Wilson. Thanks to all my local relatives, Ashyia Hankerson, Bobby Davis, Anthony Wright, William Wright, James Wilkins, Leroy Wilkins, Carolyn Davis, Carenada Davis, Alicia Davis, Charletta Davis, Martha Hankerson, and Clearthur Davis. To my entire family I would like to say thank you. I would like to thank my boys for life, Edward Dean Arnold, Tony Farrar, RIP to Timothy Farrar, Martin Williams, Torrey Thorne, Frank King, Tony Lawrence, Reginald Shambley, Rodney Debrow, David Jenkins, & Wendell Battle. I like to acknowledge everyone in the Happy Hill community that I grew up with. Thanks to Pastor Halloway at Zebulon First Baptist. To my Christian brothers that have influenced me spiritually; Eddie Brinkley, Deon Bell, George Wooten, and Kelly Hines. To my, Awesome friend and classmate, Casandra (Cece) Coley, thank you for support and commitment. To my Bridgestone family; Tony Barnes, Lee Patterson, Tony Parnell, Travis Ray, Gilbert Smith, Melvin Johnson, Samone Leak, & Craig Simon. Rest in peace to Marcellus Farmer & Joe (Mojo) Allen. To every Bridgestone teammate that I have met and shared a moment with; I would like to say thank you. I would like to say thank you to so some good friends of mine that I will never forget; Sasha Gooding, Edie Bell, April Mangum, Delta Lewis, Keisha Wilson, Odaliah Deans, Tanita Bell, Treva Herring, Janet Greene, Tamika Raleigh, Magdalene Cooper, Sarah Killen, Tamara Riddick, and Linda Pittman. A special thanks to my friend Beverly for never forgetting my birthday. To Pittman's Tax and Bookkeeping & All In One Auto Sales; thank you so much. To the staff over at Moore Realty Company, Kandie, Kim, and Arvelle, thank you for giving me my first contract ever. To the staff over at Coverall Cleaning, Jackie Scott & James Muhammad, thank you for supporting my business and adding to its success. To the staff over at Nashcombe Realty thanks for your support. To my business associates, U.S. Maintenance, NEST International, Global Facilities Management, Sharon Mason at Amazingly Clean, Benji Hart at Express Carpet Care, and Dan Bennette at Bennette Window Washing. To the staff at Universal Productions; thanks for casting me as an extra in Juwanna mann, my first film. And last but not least; thanks to the staff at Trafford Publishing for publishing my first book.

Authors Note

Conversations from a quest for divine embodies my journey through life to this present point and time. Conversations are the voice inside of each and every one of us that we communicate with from time to time. Some people may say it was the little voice that made me do it. I don't want to sound cliché but that is a very true statement. The voice inside of me inspired me to write and want to inspire others through poetry. Quest meaning a journey or in search of. And divine meaning anything Godly, or heavenly. My conversations are basically reports of a diary of my timeline. My conversations are poems which derive from inspirational, to personal, to spiritual. You will be able to witness my passion, my growth, and my transformation throughout this entire book. I start out with inspirational poems about being supreme divine. Then I will allow you to look into my personal life through experiences and lost of love ones. Between me writing about motivation and inspirational poems I got saved and found the Lord. My transformation allowed God to enter my life and **Unlock** his purpose that he intended for me. My passion has always been to inspire and uplift myself as well as others. Your passion is your desire to achieve what you enjoy doing without having a big financial goal or gain behind it. Some people prefer to be a teacher versus a lawyer or doctor because that is what they enjoy doing. Your passion is not based on money but on self reward. When you align your passion with God's purpose you will breed success in abundance. This book is my foundation and is thirty plus years in the making. We all embody a composition or novel inside of each and every one of us. I thank God for **unlocking** me and allowing me to reveal my composition in the form of poetry. This book is so much more than inspirational poems. This book inspires, teaches, and if you don't know God you will definitely learn about him. And if you know God; you be able to fellowship along with me on my journey through the spiritual part of this book. Whether a Christian or not this book has something for everyone and can uplift you through your trials and tribulation and pat you on the back in your triumph. When you read this book you should learn a lot about me and some things that you didn't know about your self. For those of you that know me will learn more about me; and for those who don't know me, will be a learning experience. Thank you again for taking the time out to follow me on my quest for divine; and I hope that you sincerely enjoy this ride.

MY PRAYER

Dear God almighty allow me to spread your grace through my obedience and anointing. Allow me spread your message that will touch the souls of those in need of your blessings. Lord bless me in favor to symbolize your power and grace and let your will be done. Thank you for your mercy; which is so enduring. Thank you for your grace through faith that we are allowed access to your blessings. Lord I thank you for continuing to bless me with the talent that you have unlocked in me. Lord I thank you for continuing to bless those that are sick and suffering; those that stopped believing in you; and those that have run astray. Lord it is through the blood of Jesus that we all have access to enter the kingdom of heaven. It is through the blood of Jesus that we have redemption of our sins. Lord thank you for saving me through your mercy and grace; through the blood of your son Jesus Christ our Lord and savior; Amen.

My Passion

Your passion is that part of you that wants to succeed in what you like doing. My passion has always been to inspire whether it be myself or others. Your passion is the glue that you will need to align with God 's purpose. There are many successful people out there and they too had an over whelming desire to excel. From Warren Buffet to Oprah Winfrey; they all were pregnant with an idea. Every successful person gave birth to an idea that they labored with or were pregnant with. Your passion helps generate that idea inside of you; until you reach the purpose for what God created you to do in this life. So many of us never blend our passion with his purpose and we miss out or fail to produce that idea or talent inside of us. If you don't allow God to manifest in your life you could live your entire life or die; without ever becoming the person or doing what it is that you were suppose to do in this life on earth. God holds the key and his purpose already belongs to us. When we discover our passion and use the key; we can achieve so much success and allow the world to see our idea or talent. For me my passion aligned with his purpose is my poetry along with what ever else that God has in store for me. For years I prolonged my happiness; by not allowing God to use his purpose in me. You got people dying every day that never gave birth to that talent or idea inside of them but had access or an opportunity through God to do so. Its like dying of thirst standing next to a water fountain, or living homeless when you have a million dollars in your bank account which you have access to; but wont use. Thank you God once again for allowing me to align my passion with your purpose to introduce poetry to this world; and through your will preparing me for what ever else you have intended for me. This next chapter contains poems designed to inspire and keep you motivated.

MY QUEST FOR DIVINE

O ne day I felt that it was time; to release to the world what was on my mind. I wanted to inspire and motivate, but slowly I started to cultivate. I went in search of supreme design; then I got saved and transformed my mind. I started to write an art was formed, my quest allowed a poet to be born. Just like a great singer that likes to perform, I am giving you everything I got when I write these poems. Like a performer giving their best on stage, my blood and sweat go from page to page. Don't wish me luck and say break a leg, if you hunger for poetry you are about to be fed. My quest for supreme has changed in design; continue to follow me on my quest for divine.

SUPREME

In life we wait for vision through time; that surely unfolds our supreme design. It's not a design from knit or script; it is a design that will definitely fit. If you fast forward your life in time; you will be in the chapter that supreme designed. Whenever your search is under way; supreme is superb from day to day. Supreme is the highest that I can be; to find the creation inside of me. If supreme is not a part of you; you can't be what you were born to do. Through trials in life we are faced with challenge, and all the while we search for balance. What I wear may not fit you; because your design is out there too. What I wear may seem extreme, but that's because I am supreme. Supreme gives me my confidence; an alliance that is my perfect fit. What I wear is not my gear; I align supreme with the atmosphere. Find your design is your assignment, so you can be one with universal alignment. My design was created in harmony; it allowed supreme to be a part of me.

ONE AWAY

I am one step away from having it all, I am one prayer away from God answering my call. I am one foot away from being too tall, I am one girl away from being a dog, I dream every night of having it all, then the nightmares come and threaten it all, I am one candle away from making a light, I am one wrong away from making it right. I am one heart beat away from having some soul, I am one dollar away from having some gold, I am one prince away from being a king, I am one lady away from having my queen, I am one diamond away from having a ring, I am one design away from being supreme. I am one good away from being the best; I am one answer away from passing the test. I am one fun away from having a ball; I am one store away from having a mall. My poetry is emotional it has it's perks, I AM ONE POEM AWAY FROM PUBLISHING MY WORK.

DIVINE

ometimes we search but never find; a quest that includes one of divine. A life fulfilled without a doubt; if you believe in finding Heaven's route. Dreams don't happen if you erase; a cat must have a mouse to chase. A clock with no hands doesn't keep time; you must have patience when seeking divine. Divine teaches time how to wait; a broken clock is right twice a day. That is so equivalent to the truth; a life for divine we must pursue. If we study life so carefully; we might discover our destiny. If your life pertains to Godliness; divine is surely a part of it. When you possess divine power; opposition will face extreme devour. To live a life that's fruitful and giving; you must always incorporate divine in your living. Accept this life at any rate; and always be willing to participate. Divine has the power to reiterate; with everlasting life to rejuvenate. We all have a quest to redefine; just make sure your journey will be divine.

THE VOICE

I never knew what God instilled in me, until he awakened the voice in me. Writing was never a challenge for me, but poetry was something that I did not see. Sometimes we have to find the glue, to seal together the talent in you. The link to talent is to render choice; and it wont seem hard to find your voice. Your voice is loyal and impartial to; the conversations that take place inside of you. Reading the word should empower you; the voice inside gets hungry too. When you feed the voice you form a pack; your voice we give you something back. For me the voice would talk to me, and I would start writing poetry. I wrote my best and got feedback, and I was amazed at how people react. When people get inspired from my writing source, it encourages me to write more and more. Now poetry is my weapon of choice, and the ammunition is my inner voice. The voice started out supreme and divine; but the voice I still did not recognize. The voice coached me while my journey evolved; the voice had always come from God. God has placed this voice in my mind, to generate conversations from a quest for divine.

SOUP

Writing poems deserve a mic, an artist words become a life. The voice of words are fed in might, that you will develop an appetite. When you are fed from what we do, our writing we call it serving soup. When you write the best that you can do, soup is what comes out of you. When you don't put heart into what you do, you don't get soup you get plain old stew. When you borrow words that are not your thoughts, you don't get soup you get chicken broth. Vegetable to soup is like words to truth, both will nurture and inspire you. Chicken to soup gives it the flavor, the flow of a poet is what we savor. When a poet stays true to what they do, the soup they serve will go into you. When you serve soup it should never be cold, a poet should never write what is not from the soul. Soup should be hot that's why you blow it, words should stay hot that come from a poet. When you have taste you write shear delight, I never knew people would eat what I write. Whether serving soup or writing poems, make sure you send quality to where it is going.

Family Affair

E motions and feeling aren't hardly the same, emotions are spare of the moment where as feelings can remain. Sometimes we lose our feelings by moving ahead, but they can easily resurface and enter our lives again. When feelings merge with emotions it can be a mere formality, love is attracted to lust, and jealousy and envy want to date casually. You see love is the cousin of lust for the most part; when the two decide to date you can't tell them apart. Emotions run fast they are quicker than the rest, feelings run like a snail they are easy to catch. Jealousy and envy should never become friends; sometimes they are referred to as the evil twins. They are useless together most definitely; it is like having a black and white HD TV. Love and lust should acknowledge they are kin, and envy should depart from his evil twin. Keep emotions far away and feelings free, and they can function independent as a family.

I AM THE FORCE

I am what MICHAEL JACKSON was talking about in the beginning of DON'T STOP TILL YOU GET ENOUGH right before he screamed; I am the PASSION OF CHRIST in the last scene. I am Denzel Washington in JOHN Q, I am Mr. BALBOA at the end of ROCKY II. I help them survive when they took out the TWIN TOWERS; I kept them afloat in KATRINA'S worst hour. I was ALI the night he knocked out GEORGE, I was MICHAEL JORDAN before the 76 points he scored. I was ROSA PARKS when she kept her seat, I was MLK when he marched the streets. I was SENATOR OBAMA before he started to run, I was Malcom X at the window with the gun. I am Fantasia before winning the Idol, I am the last soldier coming home with an empty rifle. I am everybody that lives their life to the limit, I am the FORCE THAT DRIVES THE HUMAN SPIRIT.

MY PHANTOM SHADOW

I have always dreamed of going far, I found a place amongst the stars. I count every star in the sky I see, I pray that one shines a light on me. That star that shines will free my mind and that is half the battle; when the light hits me it will comfort me and cast a phantom shadow. That shadow will always follow me, that shadow will never abandon me. At night when the stars shine on me, my phantom shadow is what they see. This shadow has been there from the begin; this shadow will be there at the end. I sometimes phantom now and again; how this shadow is so similar to being a friend. This friendship is on the ascending end; and this is the closest to Heaven I have been. This shadow has cast a light on me; now Heaven has secured a place for me. If you believe in what you dream, nothing in this world is too extreme. My phantom shadow has represented; my path in life is unprecedented. What I dreamed is what will be, my phantom shadow is apart of me. If a star should fall it would seem so shallow; it will only make me closer to my phantom shadow.

WALK IN THE LIGHT

From the embryo to the ash, the guidance of light is my path. If I believe in what I dream, my vision will all but be foreseen. When the light touches the soul the spirit illuminates, now the soul is free from darkness and the light is mine to take. To glow through faith is to grow what's right, what you plant in the day grows at night. All things are possible your belief is sight, when you illuminate your faith you walk by the light. When you walk at night your shadow will array, your soul conquers darkness so the night will run away. As the sun rises it is symbolic to light, your walk to victory is no longer a dark night. Your race against darkness is a part of life; your faith is your walk in the Christian life. Disobedience and no faith will come at a price; that is when you begin to walk outside of the light. When you get off course you should jump back on, you just got to turn the light back on. Take your time don't skip and hike, and you can return to your walk in the light.

Mind Elevation

Elevating your mind takes a different approach; living in poverty doesn't mean you are broke. Lacking in life has a new effect; you pay for that with a reality check. You can't get rich by chasing dimes; a poor man can always enrich his mind. Renew your thinking is called mind elevation, and father time has an explanation. Seedtime harvest is what you sow, and pleasing God starts the growth. Elevating to God is called having faith, some flee from God and take the fire escape. A rich man is poor when he lacks in health, a rich man is poor if he doesn't know himself. Wealth is having an abundance of health, career, life, and all thee above. Mother earth tried to show you first, your bank account doesn't determine your worth. Transformed thinking is half the battle; in this mind state there is no capital. A fulfillment believed is your evidence, and poverty should never replace common sense.

I AM I AM

I am I am what God has named; I pray every prayer through Jesus name. I am rebirth and spirit formed, I live in this world but I am not conformed. I am a new creature and I walk in the light, I consume the word that is the bread of life. I am a new recipient of the supernatural life; I am saved by the blood of Jesus Christ. I am new in spirit but my body has not changed, my soul has witnessed a spiritual thing. I am a sower of seeds to the eternal life, I live by the giving and I worship Christ. I am consistently blessed by God's grace, I walk by faith and I am winning the race. I am an ambassador for Christ and that won't change, and every demon in hell knows my name. I am delegated by God to use his power, until he returns no one knows the hour. I am I am an agent of change, and God will always know my name.

HEAVEN KNOWS

For all of those uncertainties, heaven knows what's best for me. You can love yourself you should never lust, because that can lead to self-destruct. What you hide from now you will run into later; there is a place in heaven that is so much greater. I am ready to travel my journey begins, on the road to heaven starts from within. I don't need to drive an Infiniti, on my road to eternity. Heaven has no doors but hold the key, to unlock the promise of my destiny. I have to take a moment to spare, and know that God can get me there. What unfolds awaits in time, and that begins my earthly demise. My arms are open my soul is free, but ultimately the choice depends on me. Heaven is so evident, that I can change my residence. Heaven has been sworn to secrecy; for answers that will always belong to me. Answers to questions I want to know; I will not find if I don't go. Life is the test you don't study for; you are graded but not given a numerical score. The results of your test are full and complete; Heaven holds the answers to what you seek.

WHY?

I f seeing is believing really means so much, why can't I find a rainbow that I can touch? If Love has no hands; how can it touch my heart, how can one piece out the puzzle make it fall apart? Why do birds always fly south for the winter, why do homeless people always prefer money over dinner? Why do we call it hamburger if it doesn't contain ham, are we all government related by **Uncle Sam.** Why does a raisin in the sun seem so warm and kind, why do we step on grapes to make them wine. If we all were artist's we could paint for fun, why can't policeman be artist if they draw their gun. Can I have faith without having a vision, can a blind person in charge have supervision. If we are all equals whether rich or poor, why does society tend to judge us by our credit score? If we as people are so important, why do we put people that are missing on the back of a milk carton? If gambling is bad and very extreme, why do we put our whole paycheck in the slot machine? Just like there's no cure for AIDS or CANCER, each day we come closer to finding these answers.

Homeless Resident

A living place or temporary fit, on earth my body is a homeless resident. My body is the temple for the heart to reside; the eyes are the windows that the mind sits behind. The heart is vacant you can't live inside, the heart needs love or it won't survive. A house is like the body it's a temporary space, while you are in search of your final resting place. The flesh rules the body it doesn't belong to me; the home I find I will rent it for free. The body follows the mind it can't decide, the body is homeless when earth resides. We are here on earth for a little stay, but we must decide our eternal place. The choice we make is so at stake, that's why we pray our soul to take. The body we consume is so profound, when our soul leaves it goes back to the ground. Homeless to me is not a look; that's why you really can't judge a book. When you search deep you will discover, there is so much more to be uncovered. A life with much anticipation; a homeless state or situation. Your search for a home you will derive, after you ascend to your eternal reside. Whether Heavenly trail, or Hell lane, your living situation won't be the same.

FAR AWAY

One cry from being all cried out, I must find away to breakout. The world's stress is on my chest; I'm on the opposite side of being the best. Debts and bills are on my heels; reality is starting to feel so real. Far away is what I need, far away will help me breath. The love in my life has come and gone, I feel so sad and all alone. Far away is what I need, far away will help me breath. My job just mailed me my last check; my car has just been repossessed. Far away is what I need, far away will help me breath. Broke and disgusted has no price; I want to end my own life. Far away is what I need, far away will help me breath. I asked God for help to make it right; I got on my knees and prayed to Christ. Far away seems so close, my love for God started to grow. I launched my faith and started to believe, and God has given me all I will need. I see my faults and what went wrong, **Far away is just a song**. This song my stress has heart and soul, thanks to **Kindred The Family Soul**.

My Growth

My growth is basically me perfecting and exploring the talent that God has **unlocked** within me. My talent is poetry and inspirational thought. I started out writing poems in my cell phone and saving them to my drafts. I would send these poems to some friends of mine to inspire them. After so many over whelming responses; they inspired me and encouraged me to continue to send poetry to them. I started to reach deep down inside of me, to bring out the best poetry that I could. The more I grew as a poet the more people started requesting my poems through text message. As long as I had my cell phone I could write and send poems from anywhere. Whether it be at home, or at work, or driving; if I got hit with an idea for a poem; I could type it up and send it anytime. My passion gave me the hunger and thirst to write better and get better at perfecting this craft that was inside of me. If I was asleep I would awake and write poems; and if I was driving, I would pull to the side of the road and write poems. My poems would come to me through the voice inside of me; and from that point on, as long as I had my cell phone I could type it in and save it. From texting poems to writing a book; God is really allowing me to do what he has created me to do. The next chapters include poems with a personal touch.

WHO AM I

My spirit was birthed from the motherland of Africa with streets paved with blood of those who fought with their souls exposed; in this country as a youth, I raced a marathon chased by dogs as they turned the water hoses on me; my appetite is suppressed by opposition; I ate breakfast with slavery; I had lunch with segregation; and dinner with racism and inequality; I am on the path to prophecy; Dr King told you that I was coming, my hands are bloody from trying to put back together the mirror that was broken from over 400 years of struggle; who am I in this mirror, (Obama).

YOUR DAD

Technology today is so advanced, but they don't make GPS to find your past. Facebook played a part for me, it connected me to my history. My Facebook friend Keisha had become compelled, she told me about our son through email. Forget all rights to privacy, for eighteen years she kept from me. Back then I kept track but not the score, I was senior and she a sophomore. Of course we shared a night of flavor, but I wouldn't see her until eighteen years later. After all these years she kept it hid, knowing and not telling me about our kid. She gave me a pill that was hard to take; she was walking home from school when she got raped. Then she decided to be discreet, she didn't tell her parents until after a week. She went to a place that was dark and secret, whether my son or his she was going to keep it. To connect your past you must bridge the gap, you can't destroy your past by burning a map. Maturity through age must come through time, and then one day she felt that it was time. A seed develops on how you grow it; we all played the role of Maury Povich. I guess we know how that turned out; I was his dad without a doubt. Life for us had just begun; I would never ever deny my son. We can trade time but not our youth, now that Dwayne Wilson knows the truth. If you can move forward and forget the past, I look forward to being your dad. Thank you (Keisha & Dwayne)

My Legacy

They say a good act is hard follow. I'm living each day like it's no tomorrow. I never been firm on being frank, but there are a few people that I like to thank. I would like to thank God almighty for teaching me wisdom, if you have done me wrong you are forgiven. I like to thank my girl that I put first, without the hurt I wouldn't have put God first. I like to thank the thief that stole my car; we don't know how grateful we really are. I like to thank the man who tried to sell me drugs, I should have prayed for him and showed him love. I like to thank the man that tried to take my life, now I hold on to God with all my might. People do things that we sometimes question; a lesson overcome is really a blessing. If it wasn't for those that impacted me, I couldn't leave behind a legacy.

MY MOTHER

You were like a soldier to me more than anything, how could a woman so tough be more like a queen. I watched you pray on your knees all the time, how could God take away a woman so kind. You taught me patience and how to wait, and now I know that God made no mistake. You made me laugh through some good old times, and everyday I still play them back in my mind. You fought high blood pressure and battled cancer, because you knew all along that God had the answer. Three days a week you fought the dialysis machine, and seven days a week you remained a queen. You were my inspiration, my heart, my drive, and everyday I wish that you were still alive. I remember praying for you by your hospital bed, and you would look and smile and tell me what God said. You would say don't worry it will be ok, because God is with me everyday. Now it has been five years since she passed away, but it still feels like it was yesterday. Now this poem is real it isn't a theme, God I wish she were here to witness my dream, but never the less you are still my queen Rest In Peace to my mother Maxine. (12/17/2007).

I MISS

When I think back then and I reminisce, there are some friends and family that I really miss. She started our family with the love she gave us, RIP to my grandmother Miss Emma Davis. I will never forget my mother's love; I wish Maxine could give me one more hug. My cousin Shelton was taller than me, now he rest his soul in Washington DC. Great aunt Helena was my oldest kin, when aunt Ann ran away she moved her in. I saw a lady in a house that looked like a palace, she really reminded me of my aunt Mary Alice. This aunt of mine died so young, I'm talking about Boot and Anthony's mom. He was a friend of the family that we haven't forgot, Mr. Tender Atterburry but we call him slingshot. I borrowed his looks but none of his scares, he was my biological dad but I called him Charles. My dog Binky was just like my kin, I see why they call him man's best friend. Love your friends and family everyday, and don't forget those that have passed away.

HEART TO HEART

Transitional growth through worlds apart, you can mold your clay to a piece of art. When two souls ignite to cause a spark, they both are joined from heart to heart. A heart of love is free from lust, a heart of love should value trust. If love is vodka then the heart is rum, they should never beat to a different drum. One on one they coincide, and the hearts should never ever divide. Sex should never imitate, when love is being intimate. When love is lost the heart will ache, the cost of love is a lot at stake. If love returns it renews the soul, and then you will have a heart of gold. The center of the heart windows the soul, and a warm heart should never get cold. Secure your love through every part, and you can have your heart to heart.

SCHOOL BUS

One day I will grow up to be old enough, to ride with my cousins on the school bus. To ride the bus has been my dream, I want this more than anything. I get up early everyday, to watch my cousins ride away. My chance to ride is such a joy, that I will trade my favorite toy. When I finally got my chance to ride, I had the greatest feeling ever inside, That day was great and left me guessing, did I ride the bus or learn a lesson. To ride the bus was part of it; my dream realized was confidence. Every dream that I pursue from this point out, will require my school bus to finish the route.

MY ADDICTION

If I only had two senses to touch and to taste, I could identify her smile anytime, any place. I am totally addicted and so far gone, it's like a deaf person using a cellular phone. She frequents my mind she comes and goes, she got me resembling Pookie's role. Money doesn't matter this girl is too fine; I would sell me house and give her my last dime. If her love was a car it would be a Bentley, she is about to do me like Bobby did Whitney. Her love skips my heart and goes straight to the veins; I am attracted to her like an addict to cocaine. She controls my emotions and makes me sad; I'm about to become a rehab grad. Her love is a drug that I chase after, in a pharmacy you find her over the counter. Her love is superb far better than the rest; she got me looking for her heart with a GPS. I fiend for her love and I need a fix, this is a love that I cannot quit.

TAMIKA

Roses are red and violets are blue, there is one good man in the world for you. Identical in signs and parallel in drive, vintage in comparison like a great bottle of wine. Only time will tell if we ever do meet, you are so fine from her head to your feet. We text each other to share our minds, our schedules are busy and they don't align. You are very realistic and have a big heart, and I knew that I would like you right from the start. A queen of hearts, however you play, and no one knows where the cards may lay. I took off my vest and exposed my heart, so cupid's arrow can find its mark. Your friendship means the world to me, so I am letting you know through poetry.

UNTITLED

Blame me for not being a brother to you, I had to do what I had to do, my father was never there for me, so I too wont be there for my seeds, my lust for sex is that part of, love that I never knew the difference of, my seeds don't think harsh of me, the white man is the reason why I cant succeed, what I do is my mother's joy, and she will always take care of her baby boy, sisters please don't give up on me, take my hand and walk with me, teach me love and hold on to me, so that I can be the man that you want me to be, I don't take credit for who I am, to society I am just another **Black Man.**

MY FUNERAL

I have finally made it to the grandest stage of them all, I am headlining, there is no time like the present to extinguish what is resourceful and divine, in which time captures the essence of my image as it is briefly displayed in a glistening tear drop before it is joined by saddened souls of the mourning; the morning of the dawn of reconciling, gap that bridges spirituality with reality, the alpha to the omega, the journey of transition has initiated its course of life is now flashing before my eyes, I pray that I right my wrongs a and that I have loved more than I have hated, for life to understand is to be understood, if you love me you will always harbor me, this is my time, my life, my prayer for my demise, this is my funeral.

LEO'S LOYALTY

If loyalty is my only flaw, what happens to astrological law. If Leo stands above them all, why do we take the hardest fall. Relationships seem to cause a stir, when catching feelings start to occur. Always a green light when love is a go, always hanging on when love is a no. Always giving and easy to spoil, always loving and always loyal. Born in August and sometimes in July, successful until the day we die. We put the drive in (driven) and the am in (ambition), while using adversity as the fuel for transition. Mind elevation is our food for thought, and we can't fix hate by adding salt. A leo's job is never done, the number on fire sign under the sun. July through August you cannot go wrong, its like Valentine's Day all summer long. The most attractive of all the signs, the men are sexy and the women are dimes. We don't know when to break out ties, lord knows where out loyalty lies. Take this as a reference guide; loyalty will always coincide.

CECE

God has a funny way to me, of making people seem the world to me. Once you learn your spiritual place, in your life key people he will start to place. You used to sit in a class with me, and now you don't reside that far form me. My road to God has been a drive, and you have been there for the ride. To inspire is to give a person drive, inside you have made me come alive. My feelings about you are hard to describe, I am writing this poem with tears in my eyes. Your input has kept me so alert, my heart and soul goes into all my work. My friendship for you is in cement; I am a poet that you helped invent. AWESOME was your word to say, you experienced what others will read someday. Whenever I write I keep you in mind, you were witness to my quest for divine. I guess CeCe what I am trying to say, you will always be my inspiration forever in a day.

MARCELLUS (FALLEN)

G od created us we belong to him, we are saddened when people close go back to him. Instead of sad we should all rejoice, and know that God has made his choice. I pray to God and acknowledge through faith, that my friend Marcellus has found his place. September second was like a heart attack, that's the day we found out that you wouldn't be coming back. There is no way to describe that day, when you lose a friend that you cannot replace. When you work with a person everyday, there are so many memories that you can't erase. Some people may think that this is the end, but even through death your life begins. You will always be a part of the Bridgestone family, and I know that God has brought comfort and peace to your family. Angels come to earth to retrieve the fallen, God allows us to be a part of his calling. On earth your strength was a part of routine, you also served in the United States Marine. God has chosen one of the best to wear his shield and armor, I will never forget you my friend and co worker Marcellus Farmer. RIP my friend.(9/2/2011)

MY TRANSFORMATION

My transformation for me is becoming saved by God's grace and his mercy. Through the process of me writing poems to inspire; I got transformed and renewed my thinking. I discovered my identity through Jesus Christ, and became a Christian. The Christian life for me is a life style, not a once every Sunday event. When you incorporate God into your life style; he will grant you knowledge and understanding of his word. I was able to read and interpret scriptures that I had never read before in the bible. Part of the Christian life involves renewing your mind; which is reading the bible or the word of God. Romans 12:2 says; And be not conformed to this world: but be ye transformed by the renewing of your mind, that ye may prove what is that good, and acceptable, and perfect will of God. Ephesians 4:23 says; And be renewed in the spirit of your mind. When you become saved, or are born again, God deposits every thing that you will need, in its entirety, into your spirit. God is a spirit and he made us in the image of him; so there for we are a spirit as well; Genesis 1:26 & John 4:24. We are spirit beings, we possess a soul and we live in a physical body; 1 Thessalonians 5:23. We are spirit, soul and body or sometimes referred to as Tri part. Christians that do not understand that will misinterpret a lot of what the bible is trying to explain to you in scripture. Your job as a Christian is to renew your mind daily and release, what God has deposited into your spirit, from the supernatural to the natural or earthly realm; Philemon 1:6. Not only have I transformed, but my poems also transformed from inspirational, to personal, to spiritual. My spiritual poems are teachings and scripture driven. Through spiritual poetry you should develop a divine mindset and understanding; that should not only teach you, inspire you, but show you the grace and mercy of God. These next few chapters should be a spiritual awakening.

ARE YOU STEALING
FROM GOD

C ontrary to all for a religious plight, what is done in the dark shall come to the light, Our debt to God can never be paid, just pay 10% of what you have made. Before you get your check they take out tax, what you give to God he sends it back. When you go to church and receive the word, you cannot put a price on what you heard. A common thief is a person that steals; paying your tithes is a part of God's will. Pastor's today own buses and planes, is it because the world has changed. To spread God's word don't come free, it cost to preach everyday on TV. If God called you to preach then he is a rewarder; don't worry about money because he pays for what he orders. Can God judge me if I don't pay my tithes, can I judge a preacher by the car that he drives. When I pay my tithes I'm doing my job, I can't take back what belongs to God. Pay your tithes and don't you cheat, and don't make God call you a thief.

Spiritual Health

Day and night you should meditate, in the word of God found in Joshua 1:8. Approach with grace and diligence, and prepare your soul to be spiritually fit. Hebrews 11:6 is the perfect order, believers in God know that he is a rewarder. Through the faith we are saved by God's grace, just as it is written in Ephesians 2:8. Worship God and love thy neighbor, for God gives those that seek him favor. According to Proverbs 2:5, the fear of God is your way to being wise. Exercise your body because you want to lose, the less you weigh the more you improve. Exercise your spirit because you want to gain, the more word you know the more knowledge you retain. Dig deep in the spirit to all the depths, and exercise your way to spiritual health.

WHAT YOU SAY IS WHAT YOU SOW

To say is to sow is planting indeed, thus starts the growth of sowing a seed. What you say don't take for grant, you have to be mindful of what you plant. What ever you say you should say it best, and watch your words start to manifest. Envision your thoughts and value your opinions, and you can rule over earth's dominion. God has given us free will of voice, to plant each seed through careful choice. The words of God through choice of freedom, are what we say when we sow into the kingdom. What we sow is what we speak; and that will harvest what we reap. Your harvest for earth will come from heaven, and remember this scripture from Galatians 6:7.

SPIRITUAL LIVING

When you obey God and live by the giving, you are well on your way to spiritual living, Start out each day by doing right, get on your knees and pray to Christ. Thank God for what he is about to do, his words are fact and living proof. Renew your thinking and change your mind, and focus on giving the Lord your time. The Bible tells us to meditate, in the word of God every night and day. If we lean on faith and not on sight, we start to walk a higher life. Read the word to understand, your purpose in life is in God's hand. When you read the word and start to live it, this is how God operates through the spirit. Food for thought is what you ate; now the bread of life is on your plate. If you get full from what you've read, it means you are being spiritually fed. If the word goes in you everyday, greatness should come out of what you say. Thank God every chance for being so giving, and he will provide your spiritual living.

THE BLOOD OF JESUS

God showed his grace from heaven above, to pay for our sins through Jesus's blood. The lamb of God was sacrificed, our lord and savior Jesus Christ. 1 John 1:7 is where to begin, if you walk in the light the blood will cleanse your sins. Hebrews 9:22 reveals great comprehension, without the purging of blood there is no remission. After Adam sinned the world was lost, Jesus saved the world when he died on the cross. Leviticus 17:11 describes this best, the blood is the key to the life of the flesh. Colossians 1:14 is how we win, the redemption of his blood is forgiveness for our sins. The blood of Jesus is one of a kind, and the only hope for all of mankind. The blood withstands the test of time, and defeats the devil every time. The blood of Jesus will never be in vein, that's how we know he is coming again.

SPIRITUAL MIND

You can be blessed exceedingly divine, when you possess a spiritual mind. When you become saved you are renewed to no limit, God deposits everything that you will need into your spirit. Renewed in the spirit inside of you, now you can enjoy what God has for you. People get saved all the time, but some of them fail to renew their mind. Born again Christians that are not renewed in Christ, will parallel their lives with a sinner's life. A spiritual mind holds much belief, transformed in thinking and carnality free. God has blessed you through your spirit; through consumption of the word your spiritual mind can get it. Your spiritual mind has so much worth; it brings the supernatural blessings to your life on earth. Thank God almighty for being so kind, in giving us his word to have a spiritual mind.

MY SPIRITUAL EYE

What I can physically see will no longer apply; I am walking by faith with my spiritual eye. What's in my heart is what I see; my spiritual eye envisions for me. My spiritual eye is not a part of my face; my spiritual eye is attached by faith. My spiritual eye cannot cry; my spiritual eye can see beyond the sky. Through vision I can become what ever I believe; my spiritual eye has but already seen. Through the physical eyes I had no belief; I just crossed my I's and dotted my T's. Following my faith is how I will lead; my spiritual eye is all I will need.

GRACE

A false disguise withholds the truth; the grace of God should unfold in you. God has revealed what is in his plan; so that you can unleash your inner man. Exquisite comes into your life; so that you can live without the strife. When we lose sight to understand; God sends his grace to reprimand. The fullness of God is grace for grace; the unmerited favor of having faith. Moses taught law in much discussion; the act of adultery causes repercussion. God sent grace to comprehend; when you think of adultery it is committing sin. Born again gives you the grace to succeed; in the things people living by the law cannot achieve. When you live life through exceeding faith; grace derives from a heavenly place. The favor of God is so unmatched; concealing the truth will be unmasked. Your hunger and thirst will be unavailable; when the will of God is at your table. Never forget to say your grace; when the bread of life is on your plate. The key to grace is eternal life; the divine favor of Jesus Christ.

TRI PART MAN

1 Thessalonians 5:23; And the very God of peace sanctify you wholly; and I pray God your whole spirit and soul and body be preserved blameless unto the coming of our Lord Jesus Christ. That is a very important scripture which explains who we are. Man is a spirit being, we possess a soul, and live in a physical body. God created us in his image and likeness; Genesis 1:26. God is a spirit and therefore we resemble him; John 4:24. Your soul is your mind, your belief, and is your thought process where you make decisions; Hebrew 4:12. Your body is a house for your soul and spirit; 1 Corinthians 6:19. The body is just an earthly house that holds the spirit, which holds your soul, until we leave this world; 2 Corinthians 5:1. If you don't understand this concept you will misinterpret the meaning of many scriptures in the bible. Your body which is your flesh, and your soul which is your mind, and your spirit are all separate. Flesh things go with flesh, and spiritual things go with the spirit; John 3:6. You must be born again to experience the fullness of God and to receive the spiritual benefits of the tri part man; John 3:7.

Spirit Soul & Body

If God created me in his image, then I resemble him in the spirit. Being a spirit helps make me whole. I live in a body and possess a soul. The body believes in what it sees, the spirit has seen what is about to be. The soul is where my thoughts take place; my belief begins by having faith. The only way to contact your spirit; is to read the word until you hear it. The body and soul should never combine, because that can lead to a carnal mind. When the soul and spirit do align, the blessings from heaven come so divine. The body reacts by what is heard, the spirit performs by reading the word. By reading the word and acting Godly, the spirit can heal your soul and body. Renew your mind and pray to Christ, your soul can choose a higher life. Read the word and don't ignore the scripture from John 4:24. We look like God and all his image; we must always worship him through the spirit.

Your Spirit

When you confess your sins and you become saved, your spirit is where the deposits are made. Everything that you will need while you are living, God deposits it all into your spirit. If you are saved and live in lack, it is because you have not used what you got. In order to release what God has placed, acknowledge what is in you and grow your faith. Faith without works wont benefit you, where will your spirit send the blessings to. When your soul is in disbelief and your body is in depression, they are both cut off from your spiritual blessings. Transform your mind and believe God can, and your spirit will release the blessings again. Your spirit holds everything that God has planned, and is who you really are in the tri part man.

YOUR SOUL

Your mind, your heart, your beliefs, and your goals, are all a part of the make up of your soul. Your soul is most valuable to the tri part man; your soul can contact your spirit man. Your soul is the place where you decide, when you leave this would where your spirit will reside. Making decisions is where your soul embodies, whether to join your spirit or to join your body. Joined with your soul your body rallies, and nothing is foreseen out of actuality. Your body associates with whatever is reality; your soul will become conformed to nothing but carnality. When you read the word and renew your mind, your soul will reap the benefits every time. Whenever your soul and spirit align, your body will receive blessing all the time. You hold the key for your life at hand; your soul is the deciding factor for the tri part man.

YOUR BODY

Your body the temple was bought at a price, your body belongs to Jesus Christ. Your body is one third of the tri part man; it constantly wants to be in command. Your body houses your spirit that possesses your soul; your body wants to take total control. When your body is dominated by physical senses, the soul and spirit have to be more convincing. When your soul and spirit form a team, they convince your body to follow their lead. When the spirit releases blessing through the soul, your body will experience the healing mode. The spirit and soul are two thirds away, form convincing your body to totally obey. Whenever your body gets out of line, it won't be allowed to eat for a period of time. The spirit and soul are correct in their ways, they're just teaching your body how to fast and pray. The soul and spirit should stay very close; your spirit is one with the Holy Ghost. Your body should join the spirit and soul, and let the Holy Ghost play the leading role.

Your Performance

After you are saved and you are reborn, God does not judge you on how you perform. Your price for sin is already paid; you access heaven because of the decision you made. Your wallet could never cover that cost, that's why Jesus Christ died on the cross. Romans 10:9 is where a sinner begins, that prayer and belief is what gets you in. Your spirit is sealed once this takes place, the holy ghost grants you heavenly space, God's love for us is a well known fact, how we perform has know bearing on that. How we perform is part of our job, which will only make us closer to God. If you reject God and willfully sin, your blessings on earth will come to an end. If you really love God and worship him, when you get to heaven you can perform for him.

LIVING IN LACK

The opposite of faith and under attack; some Christians are nonbelievers and are living in lack. If you are saved and living in debt; you have power that you haven't used yet. Ephesians 3:20 explains the truth; the power to exceed works in you. Living in lack blocks any benefit; that means you are living insufficient. Deficient in any part of your life; should not be permanent in a Christian's life. Ambassador's for God is how Christians are appointed; they should always know how to receive the anointing. Faith without works is always wrong; the anointing has to have something to get on. My advice to a Christian that stopped believing; transform your faith and renew your thinking. A mind not renewed will never prevail; you might end up in heaven but on earth you are in hell. Living in lack can always change; God has already blessed you through spiritual things. Reverse your lack and praise his name; God makes the deposit and you withdraw the change.

REPORT THE TRUTH

Some people have questioned why I do what I do, some refer to it as poetry I just report the truth. I don't borrow words by any means, my quality of work mean everything. Every word I write has heart and soul, I polish each word like a piece of gold. I report the truth when I write what is right; I write what God tells me to write. I report the truth while others blog. I write down conversations that I have with God. What I type inhabits choice; his words are given their own voice. If you call it poetry that's okay, God has given me so much to say. What God says goes in me best, and greatness comes out of what I text. My reports are to inspire and make us strong, they should never offend or hurt anyone. I will continue to write what God has to say, and hopefully it will inspire and make your day.

SIGN MY BOOK

M ost of the time with poetry, the author takes credit for everything. If I am the person to make that call, I feel like the reader deserves it all. Thank you so much for what it took, for you to take time to read my book. We don't say thanks as much as we need; bestsellers wont happen if nobody reads. I will be honored if you buy my book; it is gratifying for me if you sign my book. If I write the best for you and yours, I would love to see your signatures. That would mean the world to me, your signature will leave a mark on me. A mark on me and in the book, that is well worth the effort it took. If my poetry has been exciting to you; my words have found a home in you. What you take home is so much more, that keeps you in line at the book store. Poetry writing has become a hobby; I never thought that I would be selling copies. God has allowed me to elevate, now I am on the same shelves as T.D. Jakes. From motivational text to carbon copies; to Amazon.com with Steve Harvey. I thank God for credit is do, for giving me poetry to write to you. If you enjoyed this book and were entertained, please do me the honor and sign your name. This quest for divine was long and true, and I hope that everyone stays tune for Volume Two. Thanks to everyone that bought my book.

AUTHOR'S FINAL NOTE

I would like to take this time to thank everyone for reading and following me on my fantastic journey of enlightenment. It has been my pleasure to inspire you and share my passion, growth, & transformation. When I allowed God to implement his purpose in my life; he became the voice and author of my quest. Hebrews 12:2; Looking unto Jesus the author and finisher of our faith; is such a glorious and true scripture to live by. Since the transformational part of my life; God has been my consultant that I communicate with and trust wholeheartedly. Philippians 3:20; For our conversations is in heaven; from whence also we look for the Savior, the Lord Jesus Christ; is synonymous with meaning and coherence with the title of this book; which I came up with before ever reading this scripture. Through the grace of God he has allowed me to do what he has designed me to do in an enabling way to impact others. I have an eternal relationship with God and I hope to gain a long term relationship with the readers of my work. I will continue to produce the best material in writing in what God has purposed me to do; and I hope that the readers will continue to intercept and harbor the message that God has sent me to give to you. In reference to the word of God; hearers should be readers, readers should be knowers, knowers should be doers, and doers should be renewers of the word of God. Until my next quest I would like to thank every reader for your participation in the success of this book and God bless you.

AUTHOR BIOGRAPHY

From the early days of elementary school to the present; creativity and success has always been a part of his character. This Rocky Mount, NC native has conquered; network marketing, travel agency, building maintenance; real estate, and is now venturing into creative writing. It is gratifying to be able to impact people's lives; but so rewarding to be able to touch their souls through poetry. He owes God so much credit for his grace in allowing him to share his gift of poetry with his readers. His grandmother was so supportive in his early molding; to attending three church services every Sunday and praying on his knees every night before bed. His mother was and in her passing is still his number one inspiration and passion for writing. He was so fortunate to have such a loving and passionate family that instilled good values and drives in him. I guess by now this is no accident or by chance that he is writing poetry. It is apart of his design and God is utilizing him in an amazing way. He continues to thank God for what he has done and about to do; and to continue to allow him to write and inspire his readers.